LOVE AND LIFE

Love And Life

POEMS ABOUT YOU AND ME

Ziri Dafranchi

Heredita Press Limited

© 2024 Ziri Dafranchi.

The right of Ziri Dafranchi to be identified as the Author of the Work has been asserted by him in accordance with the Copyright, Designs and Patents Act 1988.
All rights reserved. No part of this book may be used or reproduced by any means, graphic, electronic, or mechanical, including photocopying, recording, taping or by any information storage retrieval system without the written permission of the publisher except in the case of brief quotations embodied in critical articles and reviews, nor be otherwise circulated in any form of binding or cover other than that in which it is published and without a similar condition being imposed on the subsequent purchaser.
For information about permission to reproduce selections from this book, contact Hereditas Press.
A CIP catalogue record is available from the British Library.
Ebook ISBN: 978-1-7398021-7-2
Paperback ISBN: 978-1-7398021-8-9

Hereditas Press
www.hereditaspress.com

LOVE AND LIFE

After all have been said and done
After life has been lived and spent
And, when we finally bid the world goodbye
Only one thing will matter...

...the love we shared.

Contents

Love And Life — v

Love — 1

1	Fragrance Of Love	2
2	Anatomy Of Love	4
3	Falling In Love	6
4	Love Lane	8
5	Summer Of Love	10
6	Lovebirds	12
7	Flame	14
8	Marooned	15
9	Rescued	16
10	Desire	18
11	Only You	20
12	My Promise	21

13	Reason With Me	24
14	Addicted	26
15	Without You	28
16	I Miss You	30
17	I Still Love You	32
18	When Love Hurts	34
19	Tom And Lisa	35
20	Love Untrue	37
21	This Thing Called Love	38
22	If Love Be Love	40
23	Love Is	42
24	Drops Of Love	44
25	Ode To Love	46

Life   49

26	Life	50
27	Born Free	52
28	Bound In Freedom	54
29	Let It Be Known	56
30	Before I Die	58
31	Who Am I?	60

Contents | ix

32	Not A Victim	62
33	The Journey	64
34	Voices	68
35	I Will Breathe	69
36	I Choose Happiness	70
37	Unbeaten	72
38	Aspire	74
39	Dreams And Visions	76
40	Passion	78
41	Be The Change	80
42	Don't Resist Change	82
43	Change For Change	84
44	Good Change	86
45	Change Not By Chance	87
46	Change Is The Only Constant	89
47	Right Is Right	91
48	Think Before You Speak	92
49	Be The Flow	93
50	Truth	94
51	Fire For Fire	95
52	Thundering Silence	97

53	Busy Doing Nothing	99
54	You Are Important	101
55	True Beauty	103
56	Self-Worth	105
57	Family	107
58	The Heart Of Man	108
59	Say A Little Prayer	109
60	There's A Reason	111
61	Only A Whisper	112
62	Time	114
63	The Present	116
64	Today I Will Simply Live	118
65	Tragedy Of Life	120
66	Live Today	122
67	Beyond	124
68	Dead People	126
69	Cycle Of Life	129
70	Ode To Life	130

Other Books By Ziri Dafranchi   132

Love

Image by starline on Freepik

1

Fragrance Of Love

As the aroma of a rose
wafting through the summer breeze
in the cool of the evening
your love, strong, warm and sweet
flutters through my whole being
serenading my soul

Its fragrance so intense
has me hypnotised and entranced
The sheer beauty of it, so captivating,
has left me as enchanted and powerless
as its fresh, invigorating scent
has energised and empowered me

A taste sweeter than honey
A feeling smoother than silk
A scent stronger, more intense
and sweet-smelling
than an exotic collection of flowers
is the fragrance of your love.

2

Anatomy Of Love

Beauty is in the eyes of the beholder
but in your eyes I found beauty
Your big black eyes got me hypnotised
the moment they caught my eyes
leaving me transfixed and speechless
How can human eyes be so out of this world?

Your face glowed as though heavenly
as I surveyed the intricate designs
of a Master Sculptor
My eyes sunk into your dimples
which deepened as you smiled
The most amazing smile ever

Your lips luscious and tender
are shaped to create a perfect pout
Sending bright sparks flying
the moment they are parted
Revealing your dazzling collection
with a teasing gap in the middle

Your neck, as a gazelle's, graceful
the delicate bridge to your bosom
Ample, alluring, attractive and shapely
supported by a perfect pair of legs
as though designed to float not walk
What a beauty!

You are beautiful, my love
through and through
really and ever truly
But if I had to choose
I would choose your eyes
which reflect your inner beauty
A beauty so incomparable.

3

Falling In Love

Time stopped the moment our eyes met
Your gaze brighter than the morning sun
lit up my soul with a warm glow
It was only a single flame
but it brought darkness to an end
and suddenly my morning broke
A new day and a new dawn

As I watched you watching me
I felt my heart silently breaking apart
Something new was sprouting
from the broken pieces of my heart
I thought my time had suddenly come
and my soul was escaping from my body
So I quickly said a prayer for the dying

I prayed that if this was death
and you were the angel sent to fetch me
that you may never leave me alone
but instead will remain my everlasting companion
Alas! My fear of death was unfounded
I was actually only just coming alive
because it was love that sprouted.

4

Love Lane

Hand in hand we walked
Down the lane we went
Two souls as one
With not a care in the world

Time simply vanished
Nothing else mattered
You and me together
Always and forever

I looked into your eyes
and my heart skipped a beat
You smiled back at me
and the whole world stood still

This thing called love
is not to be understood
We only need to cherish it
and the magic it brings

Hand in hand we walked
Side by side as one
Moments like this
make life a beautiful thing

5

Summer Of Love

The sky was beautifully bright
Lit by the brilliant glow of the sun
whose warm rays of yellow
was golden and worthy of celebration

Celebrations rent the air
as the whole place came alive
with the trees rising to the occasion
gracefully adorned in their best hues
The flowers unwilling to be left out
were present too in their numbers
delicately poised and elegantly attired
Sweet melodies wafted through the air
with the orchestra of birds performing
a magical and wonderful rendition
which serenaded the two lovers

Alone they sat
nestled into each other
silently savouring the moment
Not a single word was spoken
Not a single word was worthy to be spoken
The serenity was palpable
it was also almost divine
The perfect definition of bliss

Together as one
with two bodies merged into one
and two hearts beating as one
the celebration went on
It was the summer that love was born
The summer of love.

6

Lovebirds

Together they flock
every time and everywhere
same places and same areas
doing the same things
in the same ways
now and always

Together they perch
every time and everyday
same trees and same branches
chirping one to the other
sweet nonsense none else
but the two alone understood

Together they fly
every time and everywhere
round and round they go
all over the world they went
away from tribe and family
just to be alone together

Together they rest
every time and everyday
in the company of each other
happy to have each other
and wanting nothing more
The two lovebirds.

7

Flame

Like a fire in winter
thoughts of you kindle my heart
Burning gently but steadily
wrapping it in a warm embrace
as its flame cascades through me
The more I think about you
the hotter I burn inside
Is it love that fuels this fire
or is it just my imagination?
Even so, would you believe me
if I told you I've fallen for you?

8

Marooned

You promised never to leave me
"Love at first sight," you said it was
and I believed you without a doubt
Who wouldn't fall for love?
But was I naive in trusting you
or was I blinded by love?
A love that never was?

Following my heart, I fell
head over heels into your world
which at first glittered and excited
only to evaporate as a dream
Leaving me abandoned and marooned
in this island with the strangest of names:
NO MORE I LOVE YOU.

9

Rescued

Abandoned and marooned in
NO MORE I LOVE YOU island
you left me hopeless and dejected
Did you ever spare a thought for me
whether or not I drowned in grief
or I was asphyxiated in despair?
You cared not if I lived or died
It was always about you, wasn't it?

Alas, in losing you I gained me
Becoming stronger through weakness
wiser through ignorance and folly
and alive after my former self died
Resurrected, renewed and revived
I've been catapulted into a better life
In a new and wonderful world
having been rescued by love so true.

10

Desire

As a land parched by drought
pants for a drop of rainfall
do I yearn for a drop of you
As daily I dream of our bodies
entwined, dovetailed in perfect union
And to be awakened by your lips
delicately poised on mine, teasing and tempting
beckoning on me to take a bite

With my eyes I undress you
Spreading you like an eagle
before penetrating your mind with my rhyme
uniting it with mine in precoital ecstasy
And now let our bodies be united
even as our minds have been
Thrusting, grinding in perfect rhythm
of the love binding us together as one.

11

Only You

Roses are red
Violets are blue
Mountains are high
Valleys are low
The sun is hot
The moon is warm
The sea flows
The land is still
My heart is large
but there's room only for you.

12

My Promise

I never said life for us would be
a paradise free of trouble and worry
A perfect image of bliss
unblighted by pain and misery
But I did say we would be together
all through our journey

I never said if you walked with me
we would not stumble or fall
Tripped by trials and temptations
which to all are common
But I did say we would pick each other up
each time life knocks us down

I never said we would face no battles
from foes seen and unseen
driven by forces from realms unknown
seeking our distraction and destruction
But I did say we would fight together
so we wouldn't have to fight alone

I never said we would not be broken
with disappointments and betrayals
painfully piercing through our hearts
leaving us forlorn and perplexed
But I did say we would mend together
and be restored to whole and better

I never said we would be spared
the bitter Kiss of Death
when at Life's End we finally arrive
But I did say we would be together till the end
on this side of the Great Beyond
till we reunite again on the other side

This is the promise
The Promise I made to you
and which I will keep
Because I will not make you a promise
which I don't intend to keep
So do please believe me.

13

Reason With Me

Life is a journey travel with me
Yesterday I was and today I am
I may not have become all I ought to be
but don't let that dissuade you
because when tomorrow comes I will be
Reason with me

Sometimes it might get tough
when the road we travel gets rough
but don't let that terrify you
Walking together we'll pull through
another reason we need each other
Reason with me

Love defined becomes love confined
So let's not tell the world we're in love
or they may try to fit us in their box
Instead, let us show them we're love
as we let the love we share define us
Reason with me

We may not arrive at the same time
but if you get there before I do
your memory my companion will be
And if I get there before you do
I'll watch over you till we meet again
Because you reasoned with me.

14

Addicted

Restless I turn and twist
unable to keep still
I am out of control
Tossing to and fro like a leaf
caught in the eye of the storm

Up all night I daydream
unable to fall asleep
I am out of my mind
Every day I gaze upon you
as daily I sigh with passion

Desperate I cry for help
unable to cope anymore
I am rapidly drowning
All I need is a piece of you
the only fix for my craving

Helpless I am addicted
unable to let go
I am crazy in love
With you, the darkness
in the bright side of me

15

Without You

It was a long time ago
but it's still very fresh
like it was only yesterday
I've tried my very best
to cope with life without you
but try hard as I may
my best has never been good enough

I'm still broken and empty
a shadow of the person I used to be
I try so much to be strong
but strength seems to elude me
And when I try to pursue happiness
it is sadness that comes running back to me
leaving me empty and still broken

I think about you always
and sweet memories of the moments we shared
the things we did and the places we went
invade and envelope my soul
But the pain and agony of these memories
which in time past were sweet
taunt and crush my soul

I'm trying so hard to hold on
and not give up and surrender
Grasping tightly on the last strand
of hope in the sea of hopelessness
Not willing to let go and lose control
I still my soul
But for how long can I hold?

Nothing is the same without you
My world is turned upside down
and life itself has lost its appeal
I'm simply breathing
but I don't feel alive
Although I hate to admit it
I can't live without you.

16

I Miss You

I miss you by my side
walking down the lane
where we walked side-by-side

I miss you next to me
at the spot in the park
where we sat side-by-side

I miss you in front of me
at the dinner table
where we dined facing each other

I miss you in my arms
in the bed
where we cuddled each other

I miss your voice
the sweet melody I hear
when we spoke with each other

I miss your love
so pure and so sweet
but now you're gone

I love you so much
but not as much as
I miss you

17

I Still Love You

I still love you
like the very first time
when we fell in love
after we met for the first time

Our love so strong
that very first time
after we met for the first time
nothing could stand against it

Together we sailed
through time and space
many stormy waters
riddled with faults and failures

Many looked on
with keen interest
fearing we wouldn't make it
but hoping we would

Time and time again
through several seasons
our love always found a way
to bring us safely to shore

Today we still stand
together as one
with our love ever so strong
like the very first time

I still love you
like the very first time
when we fell in love
after we met for the first time

18

When Love Hurts

Love doesn't hurt
unrequited love does
Love doesn't hurt
love abused does
Love doesn't break hearts
being hurt in love does
When love hurts
hearts are broken

19

Tom And Lisa

It was love at first sight
Or so he thought
because the moment he first saw her
Tom fell head over heels for Lisa

Lisa was a very beautiful lady
Who would blame Tom for falling for her?
She was also vain, too vain
but Tom was blinded by love
and would pay dearly for it

He did his best to please her
and was willing to die to win her
But his best was not good enough
because there was also rich Butch
who had everything Lisa loved

Lisa was in love with glitter and glamour
but love was all poor Tom had to offer
His love did not match her love though
so Lisa chose Butch over him
leaving Tom broken and disconsolate

But who is to blame Lisa?
She simply followed her heart
as Tom also followed his own heart
Perhaps the real culprit here is love
who blinds us to what's right for us
while making us yearn for what's wrong

But, is love truly to blame?
Do we own love or does love own us?
Should love control us or us control love?
Love does what we make it do
Oftentimes we send our love away
from the love headed our way
In pursuit of love headed away from us
and in the end we're left heartbroken.

20

Love Untrue

Love is pure and selfless
unconditional with no hidden motive
It is not constraining or inhibitive
or else it is love untrue

True love is liberating and fulfilling
It is empathetic and comforting
bringing mutual satisfaction
to both lover and beloved

When love is controlling
self-seeking or conditional
It is not true love
but instead love untrue

21

This Thing Called Love

This thing called love
what is it really?
A sweet tingling sensation
an uncontrollable feeling
or just an illusion?

This thing called love
what is it really?
The food for the soul
the heartbeat of life
or just a myth?

This thing called love
what is it really?
Does it make us go crazy
and do crazy things
or are we just crazy in love?

This thing called love
what is it really?
Is it blind
making us also blind
or are we just blindly in love?

This thing called love
I really don't understand it
but I really don't care
One thing I know for sure
it sure feels good

22

If Love Be Love

In love out of love, how true is that?
I wonder if love is that fickle
Love today gone tomorrow
leaving hate to take root and flourish
where love once thrived in abundance

Is this love that I am feeling
or is it just a feeling that I'm loving?
Can I be in love or be loved now
only to later hate to love or love to hate?
Is this the rhythm of love?

Is it once in love always in love
or is love transient and conditional?
What is the point in loving or to be in love
when tomorrow we could be out of love?
Where is the love?

If love be love it would be the love
never-ending, never-failing, ever-faithful
unchanging and unconditional
as love is meant to be
But where is this love?

23

Love Is

Love is...
the breath that keeps our souls alive
the force that powers the things we do

Love is...
the difference:
between having and owning
between living and existing
and between life and death

Love is...
putting a morsel in that belly
which tribulation has made hungry and cold
to bring warmth to his soul and strength to her body

Love is...
helping the stranger on our path
who is no longer able to help himself
so he can continue with his journey

Love is...
lifting the feeble hands of him
whose ceaseless toiling has made weary
to prevent him giving up on his reward

Love is...
putting a cloak over the body
which life's circumstances have stripped naked
to help cover her shame and protect her dignity

Love is...
saying a prayer for the dying
whose life is gradually ebbing away
that he may find light at the end of the dark tunnel of death

Love is...
what we do to help another
without expecting anything in return

24

Drops Of Love

A rose
the heart
symbols of love
But what's love got to do
with a flower
or a body part?

Roses are red
so also is the heart
Red is the colour of love
but do you know why?

Life is in the blood
and the colour of blood is red
Red is the colour of love
because love is the visible manifestation of life

We cannot see life
we only see its container
Through love life comes alive
Otherwise life is dead in the absence of love
because to live is to love
as to love is to live

When we bleed
it's not drops of blood we shed
but drops of life (love)
And the drops of love we shed
bring life to lives
Ours and many others
So let's all bleed to life!

25

Ode To Love

I hate to say I told you so
but I told you so, didn't I?
Didn't I tell you
although love is often likened to a rose
beautiful to behold, sweet to the senses
that it is not a bed of roses
But that, like a rose, it sometimes hurts
when not handled the right way

Roses have thorns and thorns hurt
And that's why roses have thorns
For their protection and preservation
from those who are drawn to them
because of their delicate beauty
but who do not know their true worth
and so are bound to manhandle them

Love is beautiful and sweet
It is the essence of life
Love is the visible expression of life
which without love is meaningless
To live is to love as to love is to live

Love is not just something we say
it is something we do
Not just every now and again but always
and with not a single string attached
Love is freely given and
cannot be forcefully taken
It is something we give
from the abundance of what we have
And we cannot give to others
what we don't have for ourselves

Love is strong, it conquers all
It never gives up
even when the going gets rough
It never changes
even when circumstances change
When the night is long and dreary
it holds on till the break of dawn
Love always finds a way
to the light at the end of the tunnel
And even when our time here is done
it keeps memories of us fresh and alive
long after we've departed this shore
in the hearts of those we shared it with

We can't go wrong when we love right.

Life

Image by svklimkin from Pixabay

26

Life

Life is a gift
most precious
most valuable
and priceless

Life is a plan
a mission
based on a purpose
the reason for life

Life begins with
exists in
and is fulfilled
in life

To be alive therefore
is a priceless gift
worth more than money
Be grateful

The key to happiness
isn't in having all we want
but in being grateful
for all we already have

27

Born Free

I was born free
in captivity
Bound in freedom
the freedom to be
Who I am
What I am
Why I am

I am a captive
to freedom
Free in the chains
that define me
Who I am
What I am
Why I am

I am unchained
to be me
But chained
not to be another
I am
who I am
and still free

28

Bound In Freedom

True freedom is of the mind
Because, although the body can be bound
with chains and imprisoned,
the spirit of Man can never be a captive
except by him who embodies that spirit

Only us can hold ourselves captive
if we choose to surrender our freedom
to whomever or whatever we choose
and for whatever reason we choose to
But the choice is purely ours

We enter into life free
Free to do as we wish
(but not without consequences)
And even then not free to do
all we may want to
but only what we are allowed to
(by God in line with our purpose here)
Thus revealing that freedom is not absolute

Our freedom, the right and ability
to make choices in life,
is itself bound
and is imprisoned within
the Divine Ordinance behind each existence
So that, although we are free to choose,
we are not entirely and absolutely free
We are instead bound in freedom.

29

Let It Be Known

Let it be known
That I was born free
for a purpose, based on a plan
The reason I was born this way
the unique person that I am
irreplaceable and without duplicates

Let it be known
That I'm not here by chance
a product of random happenstance
who happens just to exist
I am here on a mission
deliberately chosen for me

Let it be known
That I cannot be stopped
by any force, seen or unseen
Nor can I be destroyed because
I am invincible till my time is up
and my mission accomplished

Let it be known
That I will remain true to who I am
even if it makes me unpopular
And I will be faithful to why I am
even if the world despises me
Because this world is not my home

Let it be known
When my time is finally up
with my mission duly accomplished
and to this world I bid farewell
that I was born free and I lived free
I lived and didn't just exist.

30

Before I Die

Before I die
let me live
becoming the who
I was meant to be
accomplishing the what
I was born to do

Before I die
let me live
meeting every person
I was destined to meet
going to every place
on the path chosen for me

Before I die
let me live
making the most
of everything I encounter
cherishing every moment
that makes up my days

Before I die
let me live
the life I am meant to live
as I was meant to live
Let me first live
before I die

31

Who Am I?

As time flies by fleetingly
and days and years roll back
Amidst life's hustle and bustle
I sometimes find myself alone
with my mind my only companion
It is then I interact with my mind
Two strangers getting acquainted

As our acquaintanceship deepens
and I begin to uncover myself
Amidst the many rubble and ruins
which have cluttered my mind
In the recess of my mind
I always find the same question:
Who am I?

Who am I?
A single question worth a thousand lives
Who am I?
A simple question yet difficult to answer
Am I who I am because of Who I am
or is Who I am simply who I become?
Will I ever know?

32

Not A Victim

I am not a victim of circumstance
the story of my conception and birth
whether they be lofty or lowly
Nor of the things I've experienced in life
whether they be good or bad
They didn't just happen to me
Instead, they happened because of me
so that I can become who I was meant to be

I am not a victim of circumstance
my origin, name, region, or race
in spite of the common stereotyping
which try to fit me in one box or another
I am not limited and cannot be confined
by anything that makes me who I am
Instead, they liberate and empower me
so that I can become who I was meant to be

I am not a victim of circumstance
although I've seen many battles
and have been abused and oppressed
I am not bent, broken, or weakened
The wars and oppositions I have fought
didn't just happen to me
Instead, they happened because of me
so that I can become who I was meant to be

I am not a victim of circumstance
my beginning shaped my ending
I am who I am because of who I was
My experience fostered my growth
I learnt and grew because of it all
My circumstances did not overcome me
I came through victorious
I am a victor through circumstance.

33

The Journey

I still have no idea how it all began
but I just found myself here
I've often wondered how I got here
and where exactly I am
what I am doing here
and also who I am
If only I knew

Perhaps I should've sought to know
before taking my first steps
Instead of simply hitting the road
wobbling, stumbling, and fumbling
in pursuit of the multitude before me
But where are they going?
If only I had asked

Perhaps I should've asked
but who was there for me to ask?
Mama, Papa and everyone I knew
were busy trying to get ahead
Dragging me along with them
as hard and fast as they could
Although no one exactly told me so
I soon figured it out for myself:
It was a race I had joined
So I thought I'd found the answer
to what I was doing here
Alas, it was the wrong answer
If only I knew then

Perhaps I should've known I was wrong
but how could I if we were all wrong?
Everyone got it wrong and so did I
I found out the hard way and almost too late
I was dangerously nearing the end
when in the end I met the old lady
who had all the answers I needed
If only I had met her earlier

Perhaps I could've if only I paid attention
instead of running along with the crowd
Anyway, Wisdom the old lady,
told me who I am and where I was:
It was a beautiful place called Life
with so many scenes and seasons
Each unique and different in many ways
but which all combined together to give
a satisfying and fulfilling experience
The experience being the main reason I'm here
Finally, I found the answer and the right one too
If only I found out earlier

Perhaps it was meant to be that way
For me to find out late before I am late
and then it would be too late
The end may be near but it's not quite the end
There is therefore still time to get it right
for me and for you
Once we realise that life is a journey
what then should be our goal?
Arriving at our destination the fastest
or enjoying the process and the journey?
The moments we have experienced
the memories we take with us
and those we leave behind
is the true prize we gain
when our journey here is ended at last.

34

Voices

Silent moment with my soul
in the recess of my mind
Silent moment with my mind
in the recess of my heart
Stilled in silent contemplation
mellowed by sober reflection
many voices abound
Whispering for my attention
trying to track me down
to lure me into their darkness
where awaits bondage and death
But the only Voice I hear
is the one calling me softly
into the everlasting Light
that leads to freedom and life

35

I Will Breathe

I will inhale and I will exhale
slowly but steadily
I will take one step after another
moving forward but never quitting
or looking back, except to see how far I've come
I will do what I can now
and not worry about later
I will keep my hope alive
and never despair, regardless of what I encounter
I will keep on keeping on
even when the odds are heavily against me

I will do my best
but I will not give up
And when life becomes unbearable
I will look to the sky and simply breathe

36

I Choose Happiness

I choose happiness
So I don't mind being wrong
even when I'm right
If in having to prove that I am right
I have to leave my brother wronged
Because I'd rather be kind than be right
What use is it to me to be right
if my brother is wronged as a result?

I choose happiness
So I refuse to defend myself
even though I could
If in having to win the argument
I have to also lose being humane
Because I'd rather lose the battle for self
and win the war for all
What use is it to win for myself alone
only to lose for everyone else?

I choose happiness
So I will leave the table
when love is not on the menu
even though the spread is tantalising
Without love everything else is tasteless
So I'd rather little with than much without love
What use is it to be full with plenty
but empty of love?

I choose happiness
Not because I just love to be happy
regardless of who suffers as a result
No I'm not that self-seeking
I choose happiness
for me, for you, for all
because I want us all to be happy.

Unbeaten

All the days of my life
they've fought against me
Opposing my every move
in a bid to distract me
from the reason I am

But not for a single day
have they prevailed against me
Because I was made stronger
by the Hands that shaped me
for the reason I am

Many times they've afflicted me
trying to steal, destroy and kill
But God delivers me from them all
bringing me to my Wealthy Place
for the reason I am

They see me and wonder
the wonder that I am
Still they fight on, hopelessly
as still I arise from the rubble
unbroken, unmoved and unbeaten.

38

Aspire

Aspire not for fame or fortune
but instead for fulfillment in life
Aspire not to live the longest
but to truly live and not just exist
Aspire not for vain ambitions and goals
but to accomplish purpose—our Why

To aspire is to direct all our hope
ambition, dream, energy and effort
towards the realisation of something desired
How in vain would we then have lived
ff we aspired for things with little value
having neglected the things that matter the most?

Aspire not to be known while alive
because of our wealth and riches
But to be remembered after our death
because of the things we have done:
The lives we touched; our legacy to the world
Aspire to inspire before you expire.

39

Dreams And Visions

There are dreams
and there are visions
Although both are different
they do sometimes come together
and become one

A dream is just a dream
a wishful desire or fantasy
which we may or may not
do anything about
than simply dream on

A vision on the other hand
is more than just a desire
It is something we've seen
with the eyes of our minds
which we then strive to bring to reality

A dream is just a dream
and would remain a fantasy
But when a dream is based on a vision
it becomes more than just a dream
And would become a reality
if we do what we have to do.

40

Passion

Buried deep down within us
beneath the rubble of desire
wishes, wants, and vain dreams
is something inside so strong
A force natural and innate
so powerful and compelling
it doesn't depend on who we are
to stir and get us up

It moves us beyond ourselves
who we think we are
what we think we have
what we think we can do
Propelling us beyond fear and failure

self-doubt and shortcomings
Helping us rise above everything else
that would try to hold us back

Its flames burning softly but steadily
provide the fuel that powers us
to surmount the obstacles on our path
as we make stepping stones out of stumbling blocks
and move ourselves beyond the limitations of self
Soaring through the realms of impossibilities
till finally our goal is achieved

This force so powerful and fiery
is a beautiful thing called passion
Although a good thing to have
we have to ensure we get it right
because it is not always right
When it is wrongly driven
or is founded on something not right
passion becomes bad:
A lethal weapon of destruction
instead of a positive force of creation

41

Be The Change

Whoever you are, whatever you do
if you desire for something better
start by doing whatever you can
to realise that which you desire
Be the change

Whoever you are, however you are
if you're not satisfied with your life
start by doing whatever you can
to make your life better and satisfying
Be the change

Whoever you are, wherever you are
if you wish for a better future world
start by doing whatever you can
to make this world a better place
Be the change

Be the change you desire
if you truly want a change
because change doesn't just happen
but is caused to happen
By you and by me in the things we do.

42

Don't Resist Change

Change
The one thing we desire the most
the one thing we need the most
so we can experience better

Change
The one thing we fear the most
the one thing we resist the most
although we hope for the better

To experience change
we must change
or things will remain the same

We all need change
but how can anything change
if we resist change?

43

Change For Change

Change is magical and mostly to be desired
A better life and a better world we all wish for
A life free of lack, worry, fear, and anxiety
A world free of hate, cruelty, and injustice
If only wishes were horses

A wish is only a wish and nothing but a wish
Since nothing good ever comes from simply wishing
a wish is unable to transform itself into reality
Wishing alone, therefore, cannot make real our desires
Or then beggars will ride

Change is good but it does not just happen
It couldn't and wouldn't result from desiring alone
no matter how strong or for how long our desire is
Instead, it is caused to happen by the things we do
because nothing changes if we change nothing.

44

Good Change

Things change
Situations change
People change
Everything changes

Some changes
lead to better
Other changes
lead to worse

Better is no change
than a change for bad
except the bad change
would eventually lead to a better change
Because change is only good
when change is for better

45

Change Not By Chance

We all desire better
but it will not happen by chance
Before some things can change
we must first change some things
or everything will remain the same

When everything remains the same
not a single thing will change
Because nothing changes
if we change nothing
leaving everything the same

For anything to change
we need to change something
Now, that will not happen by chance
Chance is not a substitute for change
So, change instead of waiting on chance

46

Change Is The Only Constant

Change is the beginning
It was in the beginning
and was the beginning of everything
As darkness changed, light emerged
and from then things began to change

Change is the changer
It is the beginning of life
from the embryo, the result of change
which continues to change
till a baby is fully formed

Change is the only constant
that never changes but remains the same
when all else continue to change
By not changing it facilitates change
helping all else to change

Change is the end
It is at the end
and is the end of everything
As light finally changes to darkness
bringing change and everything else to an end

47

Right Is Right

What's right and what's wrong?
Right is right and wrong is wrong
But who's right and who's wrong
in determining what's right or wrong?

Could right be wrong and wrong right
depending on circumstances?
Can we do right wrongly or wrong rightly
in trying to do right?

Is what you're doing right?
Is what I'm doing right?
Is what we're all doing right?
Only right is right.

48

Think Before You Speak

Think before you speak
Think while you speak
Think after you've spoken
To ensure your words are true

Think before you listen
Think while you listen
Think after you've listened
To ensure what you receive is true

49

Be The Flow

Don't just go with the flow
or you could end up anywhere
A dead-end or even off the cliff
and be left stranded or done with

Know yourself to know your why
the plan behind your existence
And be armed with direction
so you can be the flow

50

Truth

Truth is rare
Truth is bitter
Truth hurts

But...

Truth heals
Truth frees
Truth saves.

51

Fire For Fire

Hate cannot conquer hate
it empowers hate
multiplying and strengthening it

Anger cannot defuse anger
it inflames anger
causing conflagration and destruction

Envy cannot quench envy
it increases envy
deepening resentment and sadness

No problem can be solved by a mind similar
or at the same level as that which created it
No victory is possible when equal powers war;
the result is usually a stalemate and mutual destruction

Although we are often tempted to match fire with fire
may we remember that fire for fire only leads to more fire
And that water not fire is what quenches fire
even though it may not appear as fierce
or powerful as fire

Matching fire with fire turns us
into the very thing we desire to defeat
If we become the thing we're fighting against,
then why are we even fighting?
Don't become what you hate
while trying to conquer what you hate.

52

Thundering Silence

Empty vessels make the most noise
because they have nothing in them
Some speak only to be heard
even when they have nothing to say
And the more they speak
the lesser they say

Silence is golden
because it cannot be misquoted
and it makes even a fool look wise
Silence is also powerful
Because when it speaks
it is often louder than thunder

It is wise to speak only when necessary
and even then only what is necessary
Otherwise let us hold our peace
Because, sometimes it isn't what we say
but what we don't say that speaks for us
The power of thundering silence

53

Busy Doing Nothing

Beware of the barrenness of a busy life
where we are busy just so as to be busy
While in reality we are only busy
but have nothing to show for it
which makes us busy doing nothing

Some are truly busy and rightly so
and have something to show for it
Others just like to look busy
So they get busy but wrongly so
'Cos they have nothing to show for it

It is better not to be busy but still
and have something to show for it
Than to be wrongly very busy
and have nothing to show for it
'Cos it is result not effort that counts

54

You Are Important

You are unique and different
the only you in the whole world
You have no duplicates
and you are irreplaceable
Hence you are important

You were born on purpose
and for a unique purpose
that you alone can accomplish
The whole world is counting on you
Hence you are important

Although sometimes in life
you may travel rough roads
and may find yourself alone
You must never feel unworthy
because you are important

When we finally realise
who we truly are
and why we are
We will also realise
that we are truly important

55

True Beauty

"Beauty is in the eyes of the beholder"
A saying which is only partly true
True because our perception is subjective:
One sees a rose and another the thorns
What we see reflects what we seek
but not so with true beauty

True beauty is not only skin deep
and can't be seen with the eyes alone
But instead it reflects from the inside
to brighten what is seen on the outside
A beautiful character and personality
cannot be perceived differently by anyone

True beauty never fades but shines on
getting brighter and better with time
The body may change through ageing
Smooth skin becomes dry and wrinkled
A once fit body soon falls out of shape
But true beauty remains unchanged and untainted

56

Self-Worth

You are unique
One of a kind
intricately beautiful
generously endowed
A gift to the world

You are special
A rare masterpiece
designed on purpose
for a purpose
A blessing to the world

You are a mystery
only you can unravel
Discover yourself
to know your worth
A priceless gem

Know your worth
Don't settle for less
Go only where you are
appreciated not tolerated
You deserve better

57

Family

Our gateway into the world
A world full of strangers
Strangers who are strange
Strange not because of their looks
Looks which to ours resemble
Resemble but not exactly the same
Same world nonetheless, we share
Share we do in all we do
Do we know who they are?
Are they not family
whom we share the world with?

58

The Heart Of Man

"Some will hate you, pretend they love you now.
Then behind they try to eliminate you."
— Bob Marley.

How could you speak love with your mouth
when hate is what you have in the heart?
The heart is deceitful above all things
and desperately wicked and evil
But only if we let it.

Guard your heart with all diligence
because your life depends on your heart
Until the heart is right
life will remain wrong
But only if we let it.

59

Say A Little Prayer

Say a little prayer
for the down and trodden
Whose hope has been trampled
by relentless hardship and struggle
For whom living has become a burden
and death is a welcome escape

Say a little prayer
for the high and mighty
Whose hope is fuelled by vanity
which is here today but gone tomorrow
For whom life has lost its meaning
and death is a dreadful end

Say a little prayer
for the self-righteous saint
Whose hope is in piety and good deeds
but which in truth are as filthy as rags
For whom life holds a mighty surprise
which in death would be revealed

Say a little prayer
for the self-confessed sinner
Who hopes for forgiveness
and transformation by a greater Power
For whom life could still be better
and death a glorious transition

Say a little prayer
for me and I for you
As we journey through life
that we don't give up on hope
even when the road is very rough
So that after death we can live again

60

There's A Reason

Every pain has its gain
Every sorrow has its song
Every hurt has its healing
Every experience has its lesson

We deny ourselves growth
by focusing on what has happened
instead of why it happened
'Cos everything has its reason

The reason is the lesson
and the lesson is for growth
In failing we attain success
if we learnt from that reason

61

Only A Whisper

In difficult times
when trouble looms
The clouds darken
and darkness reigns

We find ourselves alone
isolated and forsaken
With our shadow
our only companion

Fear quietly taunts
Anxiety gallantly prowls
Worry steadily gnaws
Our soul a cornered prey

In Fortress Despair
our new home
We cower and hide
Death our only hope

Dying our soul whispers
a silent cry for help
And suddenly,
bright lights spark

Darkness flees
and with it
fear, anxiety and worry
Fortress Despair crumbles

We arise from the rubble
resurrecting into a new life
To discover we were never alone
God had been with us all along

A little prayer
changes a lot
It doesn't require much
only a whisper

62

Time

How time flies!
Morning has broken and it's a new day
Days become weeks and weeks months
Months make a year and it's a new year
As time flies by or so we say
But is it really time that is flying by?

Time is a unit of life
For each life there is an allotted time
Today we're born; initiating a countdown
Each moment represents life, lived or not
Every day brings us closer to the end
How life flies!

Time is money!
Invested in work it returns money
More work more money in the pocket
So we spend our time in making a living
thereby failing to live as intended
But is time truly money?

Time is the gift of life from God above
for us to spend in living as we should
including fulfilling our mission here
There are many things money can't buy
Most of all time, without which life is not
So time is actually life!

Time wasted is life unlived
Time wasted waiting for the "right time"
Time spent in trivial pursuits
Time invested in vain ambitions
Time used for greedy accumulation
is life unlived and thus wasted

Life unlived is the greatest tragedy of all
So teach us to number our days, O Lord
that we may apply our hearts unto wisdom
Because there is time for everything
A time to live and a time to die
O, that we may spend our time truly living.

63

The Present

The past
good or bad
beautiful or ugly
happy or sad
is no place to dwell

The future
bursting with hope
great expectation
and excitement
is only but a dream

The present
is the only place
where life happens
So be present
to experience life

64

Today I Will Simply Live

Today I woke up
alive and well
For this reason alone
I am a winner

I will arise
and do what I can
as best I can
and leave the rest

I will not worry
about tomorrow
what may or may not be
I will simply live today

I will be strong
and keep on moving
though the road is rough
But I won't quit

If I find myself
alone and lonely
I will not despair
I am enough alone

If none notices
or compliments
my relentless effort
I will be my only fan

When the day is over
and I lay me down to sleep
Only one thing will matter
I lived today

Today I woke up
I will arise
I will not worry
I will be strong
I will simply live

65

Tragedy Of Life

Yesterday we yearned
for a better tomorrow
But today we mourn
the good old yesterday
while today we ignore

Allured by its prospect
we crave the future
which, sadly, never arrives as hoped
But instead, gradually creeps up on us
one today at a time

Fixated on tomorrow
we neglect today
the tomorrow we lived for yesterday
As we continue to live for tomorrow
only to ignore it today when it arrives

When today is finally gone
dead and buried in yesterdays
Only then do we remember
as we mourn its demise
Undervalued till it's gone

O, Man!
Who has bewitched you?
Such that you prefer to live in a dream
instead of living the dream
By being present in the reality
that is called today

The tragedy of the life we live
A personal choice we make
with every breath we take
So we have none else to blame
than the person we call, "Me"
But it doesn't have to end this way.

66

Live Today

Today we are
Yesterday we were
Tomorrow we may be
but tomorrow isn't guaranteed

Yesterday is gone
gone but not forgotten
But some things about yesterday
we should forget

Tomorrow is not promised
Nonetheless it remains a dream
which for some will be a reality
and another opportunity to live

Today therefore is all we have
To do the things that must be done
including to truly live
The very reason we are here

Let us live today
because yesterday is no more
and tomorrow never comes
till in death we can no longer live

67

Beyond

Away and beyond I soar
through time, space and realm
Hovering over a land far, far away
beyond the reach of pain and sorrow
where I'll join the resting in rest

In times past I had lived
in a world full of life and dreams
And in living I dreamed
as in dreaming I lived
Till my night came

Then did all lights fade
as the curtain of life was drawn
and I laid me down in sweet repose
Yet, with the last melody sung and gone
in You I still hear a song

68

Dead People

Am I alive because I'm breathing
or am I breathing because I'm alive?
Am I living because I'm alive
or am I alive because I'm living?
Am I living though or am I just alive?
Is there even a difference?

I found myself in a very strange place
The sun shone above with brilliant brightness
casting a dark shadow on the earth below
Was it an eclipse?
No, it was the Valley of the Shadows
where I saw dead people everywhere

I saw dead people alive and well
lurching around as fast as they could
all very busy they had no time to spare
As I got closer I heard them breathing
Breathing so hard to stay alive
as if all they needed to do was stay alive

I was equally astonished and bewildered
at how dead people strove to stay alive
Being dead they cared not to live
but they were determined to be alive
Just to be alive
So they fought hard to keep breathing

I woke up breathing very hard myself
Was it a dream or a nightmare
or had I died and gone to heaven?
Wait, I'm still breathing
so I must still be alive

I ran to the door and into the outdoors
And when I looked around me
I still saw dead people alive and well
lurching around as fast as they could
Perhaps I'm dead in yet another dream
Somebody wake me if I'm still dreaming

I'm still breathing though
Can I be dead and still breathing?
Or maybe I'm in a strange land
where everyone is dead but staying alive
Because I still see dead people everywhere.

69

Cycle Of Life

Yesterday we're born
that Today we may live
because Tomorrow we die

So, Today we celebrate birth
and Tomorrow we mourn death
thus completing the Cycle of Life

70

Ode To Life

What is life really?
Is there a definite meaning to life
or is life whatever we wish it to be?
Is there a purpose for life
or is life just an opportunity to exist
and live however we wish?
Are these questions even necessary?

Life is a gift we didn't ask for
Every gift has a meaning and also a reason
Life is a mission based on a plan
The plan is the purpose of life
The meaning of life is found in the purpose for life
The pursuit of the purpose for life
makes life meaningful and worth living

When purpose is unknown, abuse is inevitable
A life outside the purpose of life is a life abused not lived
A purpose-driven life is a life well lived
It is guaranteed to lead to a satisfying
and fulfilling experience

If you find your life boring and a drag
Such that you're enduring through life
instead of enjoying living life
Then, maybe you're not living the life
you were meant to live
You may be living outside your purpose
Find your purpose and live by it
And you will find true meaning to your life.

Other Books By Ziri Dafranchi

Image by Mystic Art Design from Pixabay

WILDERNESS FRUITS
ECLECTIC POEMS AND MUSINGS
A novel combination of eclectic poems, traditional fables and short stories, and musings by the author with practical, applicable and inspirational encouragement. The fruits from a personal wilderness experience.

Volume 1

Volume 2
(Out October 2024)

MANNA

FOOD FOR THE SOUL

The first series in the devotional genre to combine poetic meditations and regular devotionals into digestible topics of faith, making it easier for you to choose and feast on what your soul craves.

Volume 1

Volume 2
(Out October 2024)

LIFE

A MYSTERY SOLVED

The captivating philosophical nonfiction with answers to many of life's most controversial questions. Book One of the Trilogy of Truth.

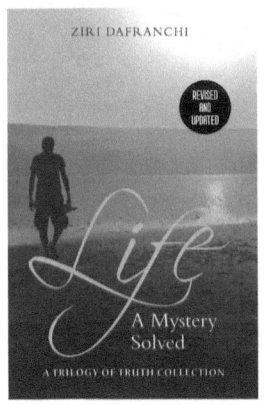

BEING BLACK
REDISCOVERING A LOST IDENTITY
The deeply revealing truth about the hidden identity of some of today's Black people. Book Two of the Trilogy of Truth.

PAGAN WORLD
DECEPTION AND FALSEHOOD IN RELIGION
The bold revelation about religion based on the present concept as a human rather than divine invention. Book Three of the Trilogy of Truth.

www.ingramcontent.com/pod-product-compliance
Lightning Source LLC
Chambersburg PA
CBHW021111080526
44587CB00010B/475